High-Tech Science

HOW DOES A TOUCH SCREEN WORK?

Leon Gray

WAYLAND

First published in 2015 by Wayland
Copyright © Wayland 2015

Wayland
338 Euston Road
London NW1 3BH

Wayland Australia
Level 17/207 Kent Street
Sydney, NSW 2000

Produced for Wayland by Calcium
Design by Simon Borrough

Picture Acknowledgements:
Cover: Shutterstock: Perig. Inside: Dreamstime: Anyaivanova 21, Gary
Arbach 38, Darren Baker 9, Beaniebeagle 7, Emanuel Corso 35, Piero
Cruciatti 40, Dobphoto 28, Edbockstock 5, Evolution1088 43, Fabinus08
18, Hustgh 8, Jhanganu 36, Antonio Jodice 32, Joeravi 20t, Leloft1911 4,
Lenutaidi 11, Manaemedia 15, 41r, Oleksiy Mark 44, Mishoo 34, Moophoto
45r, Outline205 24, Vickie Priestley 22, Anatoly Tiplyashin 42, Tupungato
33, Wavebreakmedia 27, Robert Wisdom 23; Shutterstock: 1, Auremar 31,
Bloomua 14, Goodluz 26, Yury Kosourov 12, Kurhan 19b, Lucky Business 6,
30, MJTH 29, Michael Jung 16, PILart 20b, Samuel Borges Photography 19t,
Twobee 10, Alberto Pérez Veiga 13b, Tianxi Wang 13t; Wikimedia Commons:
Maximilien Brice 17, Matt Buchanan 37, Comixboy 41l, GRPH3B18 24–25,
Medvedev 45l, Okno 39.

A catalogue record for this book is available from the British Library

ISBN: 978 0 7502 9079 1

Printed in China

Wayland is a division of Hachette Children's Books,
an Hachette UK company.
www.hachette.co.uk

CONTENTS

CHAPTER ONE:
WHAT IS A TOUCH SCREEN?

Touch screens are visual displays that people use to control a range of electronic gadgets, from games consoles and tablet computers to smartphones and satellite navigation (sat-nav) systems.

These touch-screen kiosks speed up ticket sales at a train station.

Using touch screens

Touch screens have changed the way people use electronic equipment. They make using devices much easier because you can control the computer directly on the display. Instead of using buttons, a mouse or a keyboard, you can simply touch, tap and swipe the screen.

Finger control

Most touch-screen devices work by sensing the movement of the user's fingers on a flat screen. As the user swipes or taps the screen, the computer turns these finger movements into commands. These commands control icons on the screen. For example, a tap on the screen might click on an icon and a swipe might zoom in on an object on the screen.

PEN COMMAND

Some touch-screen devices
work by using a pen-shaped
stylus or digital pen to control
the device. These tools work
in exactly the same way as your
fingers — they input commands
by tapping and drawing on
the screen of the device.

You can use a stylus
to tap in or 'write'
commands on some
touch-screen devices.

Old and new

Most people think that the touch screen is a modern
technology. In fact, the first touch screen was invented
in the 1970s. It was used to control the computers at the
European Organization for Nuclear Research (CERN;
see page 17). Today, touch screens are common in many
everyday electronic gadgets, such as personal digital
assistants (PDAs), games consoles, smartphones and
personal computers (PCs). Let's find out more about the
technology that makes touch screens work.

TOUCH-SCREEN TECHNOLOGIES

Most people take touch screens for granted when they use smartphones, tablets and other electronic devices. However, touch screens are packed with a lot of amazing technology.

Under pressure

Some devices use resistive touch screens to sense touch. Resistive touch screens consist of a flat glass surface coated with two main layers. One layer is made up of a conductive material, which means that it conducts electricity very well. The second layer consists of a resistive material, which does not conduct electricity very well. Spacers between the conductive and resistive layers separate them so that they do not touch.

Resistive touch screens rely on finger pressure to control the device.

Contact point

When you switch on a smartphone or a tablet computer that has a resistive touch screen, electricity flows through the conductive and resistive layers. Since the two layers are separate, nothing happens. However, when you use your finger or a stylus to put pressure on the screen, the two layers make contact. The computer in the device measures the change in electricity at the contact point. This tells the computer to make something happen, for example, to open an app or zoom in on something on the screen.

Precise device

Resistive touch screens work under pressure from almost any hard object. You can use your finger or a stylus to control the device as long as you press hard enough on the screen. Since the conductive and resistive layers pinpoint the exact contact point, resistive touch screens are very accurate but they do not respond to light touches.

You can press one of the icons on this touch-screen phone to check e-mail, send a text message or make a call.

SCREEN PROTECTION

The top of the touch screen — the part you actually touch to control the device — is usually a flat glass or plastic surface. This part of the touch-screen device is covered with a scratch-resistant substance to prevent the screen from being damaged.

CHANGING CHARGES

Did you know that some touch screens actually transfer electricity to your fingers when you touch them? These touch screens are called capacitive touch screens. They work by storing and releasing electrical charges. Capacitive touch screens work using only finger touch. You cannot use a stylus on a capacitive screen because it cannot pick up electrical charge from the screen.

Apple's iPod Touch uses capacitive screens for touch control.

Charge transfer

Capacitive touch screens work by storing electrical charge in a metallic layer within the glass screen. When a user touches the screen, his or her finger picks up some of this electrical charge. As a result, the electrical charge on the capacitive layer of the screen decreases.

Electric circuits

The device measures the drop in electrical charge using four electronic circuits – one at each corner of the screen. The computer in the touch-screen device figures out the difference in electrical charge at each corner. It then uses this information to calculate exactly where the user's finger touched the screen. Just like the resistive touch screen, a capacitive touch screen measures the change in electrical charge at the contact point to make something happen, such as pressing an icon to open an app.

Light touch

Capacitive touch screens are very sensitive. You can swipe across the screen with the lightest touch to get a response. The downside of capacitive touch screens is that they are less precise than other types of touch screen.

TOUCH-SCREEN DRIVERS

Every touch-screen device has a computer program called a touch-screen driver. The driver is computer code that translates the information from the touch screen into a command that the computer can understand. This command tells the computer what to do.

Many electronic gadgets now work using capacitive touch screens.

WAVE MOTION

Some touch screens work using sound waves that flow across the surface of the glass display. These touch screens are called surface acoustic wave (SAW) touch screens.

Your fingers absorb sound waves when you touch a surface acoustic wave (SAW) touch screen.

Sound signals

SAW touch-screen devices work by using an electronic part called a transducer. A transducer changes energy from one form into another. When you switch on a SAW touch-screen device, the transducer changes electrical power from the device into sound energy. This sound energy then travels across the surface of the glass as sound waves.

Two transducers

SAW touch-screen devices actually contain two transducers. One of these transducers is a transmitting transducer. It sends the sound signals across the glass screen of the device. The second transducer is the receiving transducer. This transducer detects these sound waves and converts them back into electrical signals.

Disturbing the waves

When someone touches the surface of a SAW touch screen, some of the sound waves flowing across the glass screen are absorbed. The receiving transducer registers this change to find the touching point on the screen. This sends a command to the computer in the touch-screen device to tell it what to do.

Some high-tech smart televisions now come with interactive SAW touch-screen technology.

LIGHT BEAMS

Some touch-screen devices work using a grid of infrared light. The infrared light is created by electronic parts called light-emitting diodes (LEDs). LEDs are like tiny light bulbs that light up to provide a source of light.

LEDs

Light-emitting diodes are widely used in electronic equipment to do many different tasks. They are often used as flashing warning lights in alarm systems but they can also be found in torches and traffic lights. LEDs last much longer than normal light bulbs and they are small enough to fit in tiny electrical circuits. This makes them perfect for use in touch-screen devices.

LEDs are commonly used as light sources in electronic circuits.

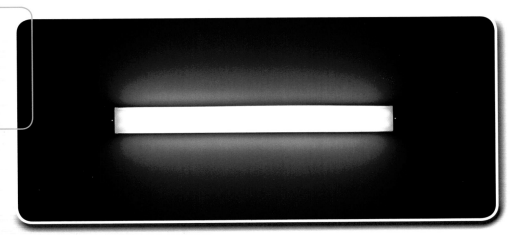

Scientists hope to use different light sources, such as neon lights, to power future touch-screen devices.

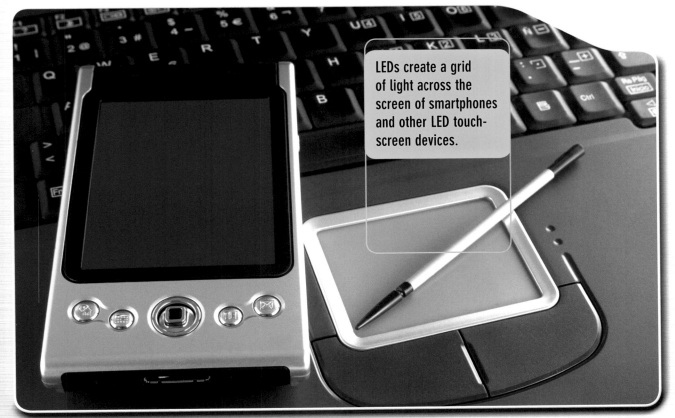

LEDs create a grid of light across the screen of smartphones and other LED touch-screen devices.

Light grid

The LEDs in some types of touch-screen device work using infrared light. They are placed along two adjoining sides of the screen. This creates a grid of light across the display. Light detectors on the opposite edges of the screen pick up the light beams as they travel across the surface of the glass.

Disturbing the light

When someone touches the screen of a touch-screen device fitted with LEDs, the light grid is disturbed. The light detectors register the change in the light signal to figure out the touching point on the screen. This feeds back to the touch-screen driver to give the computer a command, telling it what to do.

OPTICAL IMAGING

Optical touch screens are a new development in touch-screen technology. These touch screens use tiny cameras around two corners of the screen. The cameras detect objects moving close to the surface of the display.

Optical (Infrared Optical Imaging)

Active and passive

Optical touch screens can be either 'active' or 'passive'. In active optical touch screens, the cameras placed around the touch screen point at a light source. This is usually an infrared LED (see pages 12–13). In passive optical touch screens, the cameras detect light bouncing off a special reflective surface on the other side of the screen.

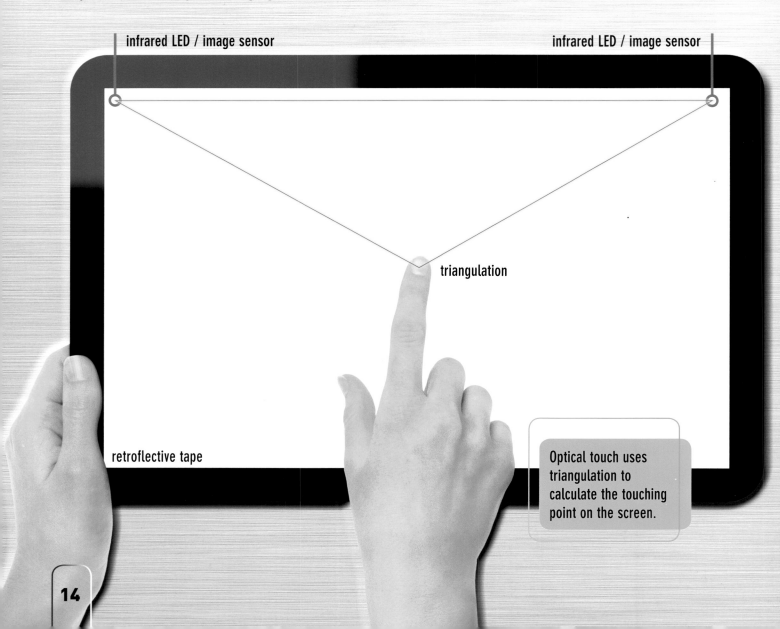

infrared LED / image sensor

infrared LED / image sensor

triangulation

retroflective tape

Optical touch uses triangulation to calculate the touching point on the screen.

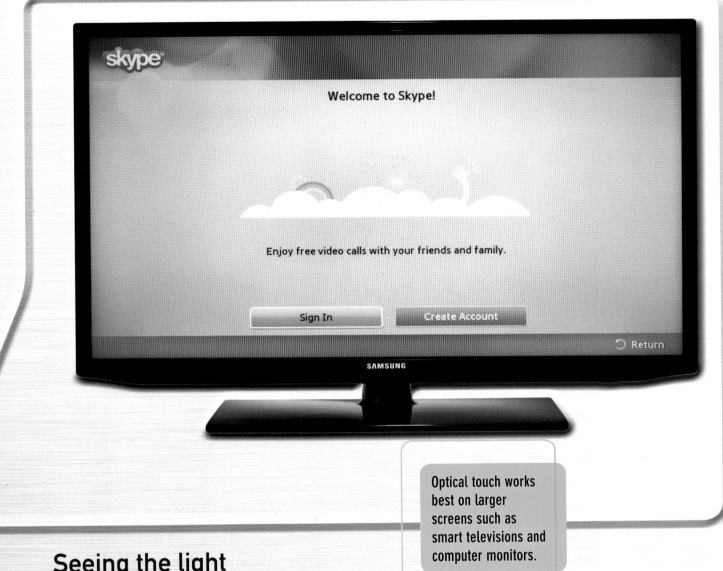

Seeing the light

When someone uses an optical touch screen, the cameras detect the change in light across the screen to figure out the touching point. This feeds back to the touch-screen driver to give the device's computer a command to do something.

Seeing shadows

The real advantage of optical touch screens is that they can detect a 'touch' without the user actually making contact with the screen. This works because the cameras pick up shadows of objects, such as the user's finger, moving near the display.

Optical touch works best on larger screens such as smart televisions and computer monitors.

BACKGROUND LIGHT

One of the main problems with optical touch screens is that normal background light can stop them working properly. In bright sunlight, for example, the cameras may not detect light from the LED light source and the touch screen can fail.

CHAPTER TWO:
TOUCH SCREENS THROUGH TIME

Most early touch-screen devices were developed for special uses, such as nuclear research and air traffic control. Over time, touch screens became easier and cheaper to build. Very quickly they started to appear in a huge range of everyday items such as cash registers, games consoles, PCs and smartphones.

Passengers can check in to their flights using a touch-screen kiosk.

Early touch screens

The touch screens that people use each day developed from research carried out by scientists and inventors in the late 1960s. In the early 1970s, Bent Stumpe and Frank Beck – two engineers at CERN in Switzerland – designed the first touch-screen device. By 1973, CERN had manufactured and begun using the first touch-screen computer.

Car computer

Soon, other industries started to look at touch-screen technology. In the early 1980s, General Motors built the Electronic Control Center (ECC). The company designed the ECC with a touch screen so drivers could control systems such as air conditioning and heating in their cars. The ECC met with little success, however, because the repair costs were too high.

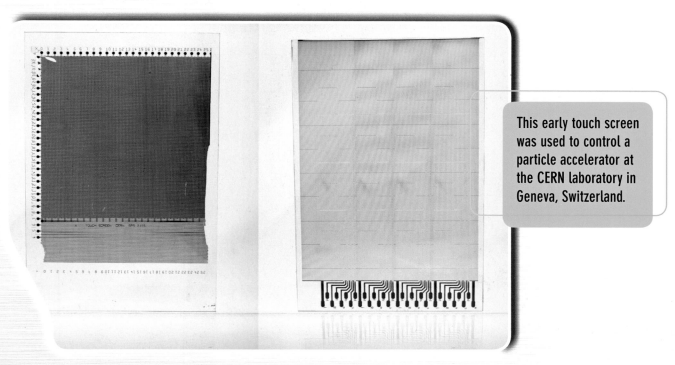

This early touch screen was used to control a particle accelerator at the CERN laboratory in Geneva, Switzerland.

Touch control

Stumpe and Beck's touch-screen computer was used to control a particle accelerator, which is a machine used to study atoms – the tiny particles that make up matter. Before the invention of the touch screen, the scientists operated the particle accelerator using thousands of buttons, knobs and switches. The touch-screen computer made controlling the particle accelerator much simpler, using fewer buttons on an easy-to-use screen. The CERN touch screen was a huge success and was used for more than 20 years.

CASH REGISTER CONTROL

An inventor named Gene Mosher demonstrated the first touch-screen cash register, called ViewTouch, in 1986. His invention became a commercial success. Today, most cash registers work using similar touch-screen technology (see pages 28–29).

THE DEVELOPMENT OF TOUCH SCREENS

The first touch-screen devices were at the cutting edge of science and technology. As a result, they were expensive, so researchers and inventors protected their products with patents.

Patent protected

When an inventor comes up with an idea for a new product, he or she can protect the invention with a legal document, called a patent. A patent covers everything about the product, from how it works to how it is manufactured. Once an invention is protected by a patent, other people cannot copy the idea and only those with the patent, are allowed to make and sell the invention worldwide.

A growing market

When touch screens were first developed, inventors took out patents to protect their products. Most of these patents ran out by the start of the twenty-first century. This meant that anyone with the technological know-how could develop touch screens. So touch-screen technology developed very quickly. As a result, touch screens have become part of many electronic gadgets.

Touch screens are now used to operate safes, doors, lifts and many other pieces of machinery.

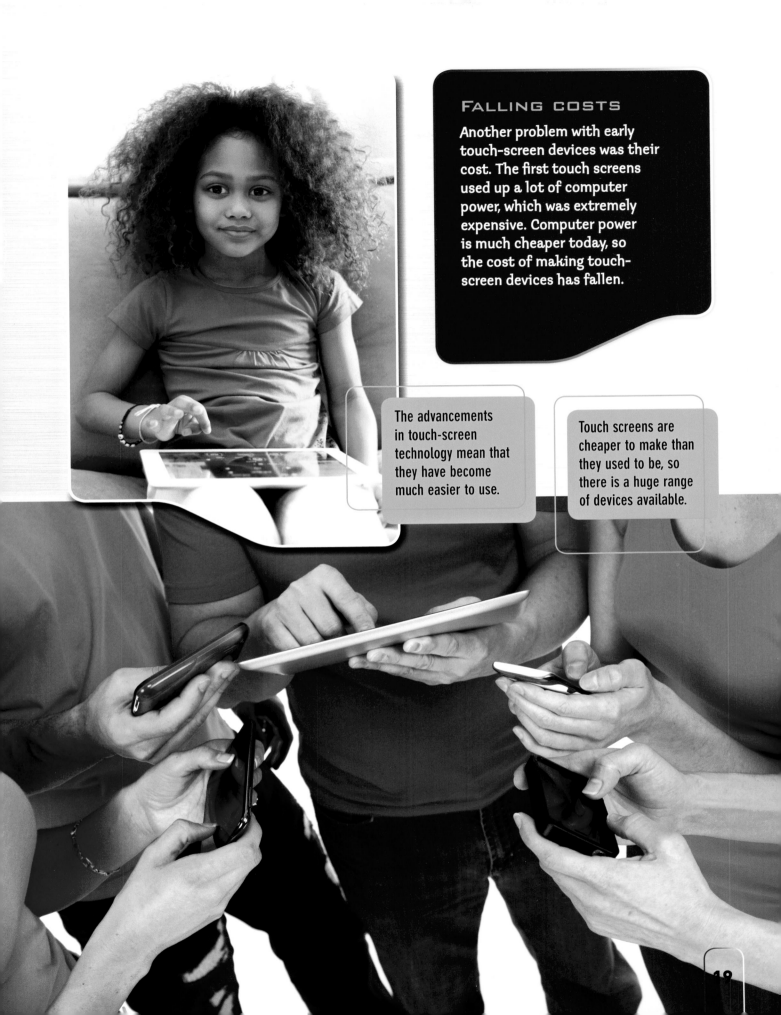

FALLING COSTS

Another problem with early touch-screen devices was their cost. The first touch screens used up a lot of computer power, which was extremely expensive. Computer power is much cheaper today, so the cost of making touch-screen devices has fallen.

The advancements in touch-screen technology mean that they have become much easier to use.

Touch screens are cheaper to make than they used to be, so there is a huge range of devices available.

BUILDING TOUCH SCREENS

You may use touch-screen technology every day but have you ever wondered what goes into building touch screens?

Building blocks

The main building blocks of all touch-screen devices are the display, which you touch to control the device; the sensor system, which detects any contact on the display; and the driver software, which is a computer program that tells a computer in the device what to do.

Apple Computers develops ideas for new touch-screen devices from its headquarters in California, USA.

Layering up

In most touch screens, the display is a flat screen made from glass or a type of hard plastic called polyester. In most touch screens, the underside of the plastic screen is coated with a metallic layer. The base of the display consists of another glass or plastic screen. The top of this screen is coated with the same clear metallic layer.

The electronic components of a touch display are built in a series of layers sandwiched between a flat glass and a plastic screen.

Research scientists test all touch-screen devices before they are put into production.

Screen sandwich

The two screens press together to form a sandwich but the two metallic layers are held apart using sticky spacers. The gap between the layers is very thin. The two metallic layers touch only when the screen is pressed with a stylus or a person's finger. This sends a message to the touch-screen driver. This is a computer program that tells the touch-screen device what to do.

IN THE CLEAR

The metallic layers in most touch screens consist of a rare metal called indium, which is mixed with oxygen, and another metal called tin. Like all metals, indium is a conductor. However, the indium compound is unusual because it is transparent. This makes it perfect for touch-screen use.

CHAPTER THREE:
TOUCH-SCREEN INTERACTION

Ergonomics is the science of making machines easier for people to use. Touch screens use ergonomics to improve the way people work with computers, smartphones, video games and other electronic equipment.

In control

Before touch screens, most people pressed buttons or used a mouse and keyboard to control computers and other electronic equipment. Today, you can control the same equipment using your fingers, a stylus or a digital pen.

People use a stylus to play on devices such as a Nintendo DS.

Fingers and pens

Resistive touch screens work as long as the two metallic layers in the glass display make contact. This means you can use your fingers, a stylus or pen to press on the display. The screen registers the touching point when the metal layers touch. SAW, infrared and optical touch screens work in the same way, using almost any type of input to register a touch on the screen.

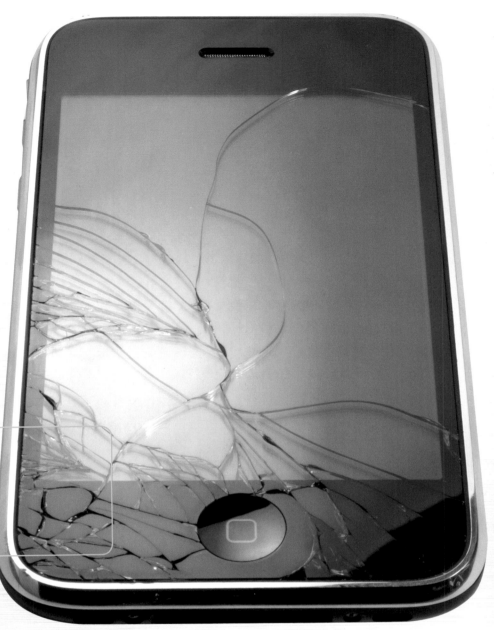

Touch screens are tough but the glass display can break if you drop the device on a hard surface.

SMEARY SCREENS

Capacitive touch screens do have some drawbacks. One problem is the thin film of skin oil that smears the screen as you rub your finger across it. Many touch screens now include an oil-resistant film to coat and protect the screen.

Capacitive control

Capacitive touch screens are different. These devices rely on the human body to conduct some of the electrical charge away from the screen. Capacitive touch screens will work only when you use your fingers to control them. One of the main advantages of capacitive touch screens is ergonomics. Users feel they can connect with the device directly, so they are often easier to use and seem more responsive.

MULTITOUCH SCREENS

Modern touch screens allow people to use more than one finger at a time to control computers and other electronic equipment. These screens are called multitouch screens and they are changing the way people interact with these devices.

The first multitouch screen

Multitouch research began in the early 1980s at the University of Toronto in Canada. Scientists there built a touch screen that consisted of a frosted glass panel with a camera behind it. The researchers used one or more fingers to move over the screen. Each finger touch showed up on the camera as a dark spot, which registered as a command on the computer connected to the screen.

Multitouch research

The next step in the development of multitouch screens came in the 1990s, when a group of scientists published a report on the new technology. They described a touch screen that could be controlled with taps, swipes, and even a 'virtual' touch-screen keyboard.

Spreading and pinching your fingers zooms in and out on parts of a multitouch screen.

These diagrams show the 'gestures' used to control multitouch devices such as Apple's iPhone and iPad.

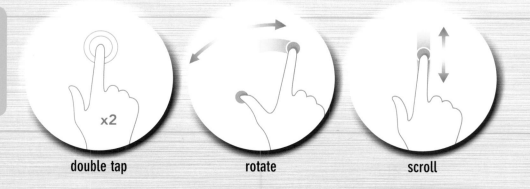

double tap   rotate   scroll

Modern multitouch

Several companies have tried to develop multitouch screens. The US company Apple Computers led the way with their high-tech smartphone, called the iPhone. Apple released the first iPhone in 2007. Three years later, the company released the first multitouch tablet computer, the iPad.

MULTITOUCH CONTROL

Apple's iPhone and iPad are controlled using specific finger movements. These include 'pinching' the screen with the thumb and index finger to zoom in on the display and 'spreading' the screen in the opposite direction to zoom out. These movements are called multitouch gestures.

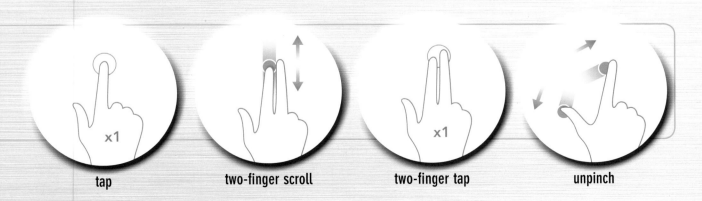

| tap | two-finger scroll | two-finger tap | unpinch |

PLUS POINTS

Touch-screen devices are replacing PCs and other electronic equipment that rely on a keyboard, buttons or a mouse. There are many advantages to using touch-screen control. Let's find out what they are.

You do not have to be an expert to use a touch-screen device.

Ease of use

Touch-screen technology is easy to work – the user simply points at what he or she wants to select. For many people, being able to touch or tap a screen is more natural than using a keyboard and a computer mouse. Touch-screen technology makes devices faster and more ergonomic (see pages 22–23). Young children and older people in particular, who do not use computers very often, can quickly learn how to use different touch-screen devices.

First-time users

A touch screen displays all the options, guiding the user through each step. This makes touch screens perfect for first-time or one-off use, for example, in a kiosk (see pages 28–29). People who have disabilities may find it difficult to use a keyboard and mouse, so touch screens are easier for them to use.

Space savers

Touch screens save space because there is no need for a monitor, keyboard, mouse and cables. This is important in a workplace where space is valuable.

Many touch-screen devices are small and light enough to use on the move.

TAKING CARE

A touch screen is tougher and more reliable than a keyboard and mouse. This makes touch screens ideal for use in public areas, such as libraries. The glass display is easy to clean and can be coated with special films to prevent damage by dust and grease.

CHAPTER FOUR:
TOUCH SCREENS IN ACTION

GPS touch-screen devices have revolutionised the way people travel.

Touch screens have many uses in our lives. Many people now use touch-screen devices such as smartphones, sat-nav units and tablet PCs. Some people use touch-screen technology without even realising it.

Cash registers

One of the first consumer uses for touch screens was in cash registers. The first cash register was developed in 1986 and worked with an early Atari computer. At the time, this was cutting-edge technology. Today, touch-screen cash registers are common. They make the sales process quick and easy for the customer and the sales assistant.

Kiosks

Self-service kiosks are one of the most popular uses for touch-screen technology. These interactive devices provide 24-hour customer service because they do not rely on a member of staff to serve the customer. Touch-screen kiosks are user-friendly. They provide the user with choices at each step, guiding them through the sales process. Many people now use touch-screen technology to purchase tickets at cinemas and bus and train stations.

TOUCH-SCREEN ADVERTISING

Touch-screen advertising panels encourage people to find out about products by engaging with the display. They can prompt the user to play games and complete surveys, which help companies learn more about the people to whom they wish to sell their products.

Bank ATMs

Another common consumer use for touch-screen technology is automated-teller machines (ATMs). People use ATMs to check their bank balance and withdraw cash by tapping on a series of icons on the screen. Touch screens are ideal for this purpose because they are easy for people to work and can stand up to heavy use.

People use touch-screen ATMs for banking services such as cash withdrawals.

AT WORK

Computer touch screens are perhaps the most common use of touch-screen technology in the workplace. However, there are many other applications in other industries, ranging from medicine to manufacturing.

Touch tools

Touch screens are common in the workplace because they are so easy to use. They allow people to do their jobs quickly and more efficiently with fewer mistakes and less training. Touch screens can withstand heavy use and they are easy to clean and maintain.

Medicine

Touch screens are used in lots of medical equipment. Surgeons use interactive touch screens to explore images of the inside of a patient's body to help them perform complex surgery. Patients also use touch computers (see page 38–39) to fill out surveys that help doctors diagnose illnesses.

Touch-screen sat-nav systems provide an easy way to navigate while driving a car.

Factory workers no longer need to learn how to operate several different machines. Instead, they can follow the prompts on a touch screen.

FINDING THE WAY

Touch screens are standard in the sat-nav equipment found in modern cars. Since the touch screens are easy to use, they allow drivers to find their way on the move. Pilots also rely on similar touch-screen technology to keep aeroplanes on course during flights.

Manufacturing

Factories often use touch screens to help automate manufacturing. Before touch screens, workers used machines with many buttons, knobs and switches. It took a long time to learn how to use these complex machines. Today, touch-screen displays make the process much easier.

GAMES CONSOLES

Touch screens are ideal for games consoles. They make gaming interactive and games easy to play. Handheld touch-screen games consoles are now common. Many people also like to download apps and play games on their smartphones, tablets and touch computers.

Sony's PlayStation Vita uses a multitouch capacitive touch screen as well as traditional controls to play games.

Early advances

The Japanese company Sega tried to build a touch-screen control for a games console in the 1990s. This early attempt did not succeed because touch-screen technology was too expensive. It took another ten years before touch-screen gaming became a reality.

Arcade games with huge multitouch screens are popular in many countries, such as Japan.

Nintendo DS

The Nintendo DS was the first handheld games console to offer touch-screen control using a stylus. This device was released for sale in 2004 and has since sold more than 153 million units. The Nintendo DS works using a resistive touch screen. By putting pressure on the screen, the user can control the gaming action.

Arcade games

Touch screens are also common in the video games found in amusement arcades. Arcade games' touch screens can be small or large and they are made from tough glass to withstand heavy use. Touch screens are easy to use, so anyone can use the controls to play these games.

GAMING APPS

More than 60 per cent of all app downloads on smartphones and tablets are games. These devices offer high-definition and interactive gaming at a fraction of the cost of traditional consoles, such as the Nintendo Wii and Microsoft Xbox.

SMARTPHONES

Smartphones made touch-screen technology an everyday term. Before touch screens, people pressed tiny buttons to make calls, send messages and surf the Internet. Today, many smartphones work by touching and interacting with icons on the screen.

Touch-screen technology is standard on most smartphones.

A touch-screen mobile

The first touch-screen mobile phone, IBM's Simon Personal Communicator, came onto the market in 1994. The phone combined the features of a PDA – such as messaging and a calendar – with voice calls.

Ericsson smartphone

The Ericsson R380 was the first touch-screen mobile phone to be sold as a 'smartphone'. It also combined the functions of a PDA and mobile phone, but it worked like a computer, using an operating system called Symbian.

Apple iPhone

Apple Computers revolutionised touch-screen technology in 2007 with the release of the iPhone. This device included a large capacitive touch screen. It allowed people to interact with the iPhone using multitouch finger control (see pages 24–25).

iPhone control

Every time you touch an iPhone's screen, it sends electrical signals to the phone's microprocessor. The processor is the iPhone's 'brain' and tells the device what to do. For example, it converts a finger 'spread' into a command that the processor recognises to zoom in on the screen.

PHONE FEATURES

Apple has released several versions of the iPhone. Each version has come with new features, such as Global Positioning System (GPS) sat-nav, a camcorder and voice control. Users can also choose from thousands of different apps to add new features to their phones.

Smartphones such as this HTC Android handset use capacitive multitouch screens to make calls, send text messages and browse the Internet.

TABLETS

Tablet computers, or tablets for short, are all-in-one mobile computers that do not use normal keyboards and mouses for control. Most rely on large touch screens, finger or stylus control and a virtual keyboard.

Amazon's Kindle Fire is a tablet version of its popular e-book reader, with a 17.5-cm (7-inch) multitouch display.

The first tablets

Intel introduced the first tablet, the WebPAD or Intel Web Tablet, in 1999. Two years later, Microsoft Corporation developed special software to run tablet computers. Early tablets running on Microsoft software had resistive touch screens and needed a stylus or pen for control. Virtual keyboards did not exist at the time, so many early tablets also included a removable keyboard.

Next generation

The design of modern tablets has followed in the footsteps of touch-screen smartphones. They combine the processing power of a normal PC with the smartphone's ease of use. They use capacitive touch screens with multitouch finger control and virtual keyboards to make them easy to use. These tablets represent a new type of computing on the move.

Handwriting recognition

Some modern tablets still use a stylus for control and include handwriting recognition software instead of a keyboard. This involves writing on the surface of the screen with a digital pen. The tablet converts the writing into text on the screen. Handwriting recognition software has been around for a long time. It is not very accurate, however, and most people prefer to type using a physical or virtual keyboard.

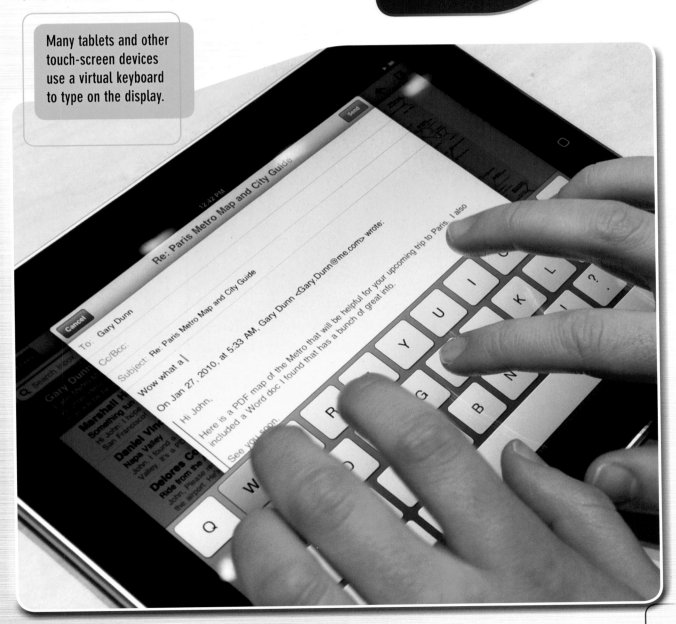

Many tablets and other touch-screen devices use a virtual keyboard to type on the display.

TOUCH COMPUTERS

Modern computing has come full circle with the development of touch computers. These computers are conventional desktop PCs with interactive touch-screen monitors.

Full circle

Touch computers are normal desktop PCs that combine a multitouch monitor with a keyboard and mouse. Touch computers grew out of the popularity of smartphones and tablets. These devices also have the added processing power of a normal computer.

Different devices

Some touch computers are all-in-one touch-screen PCs. All the computer parts, such as the processor and hard drive, are built into the touch-screen display. You can also buy a touch-screen display and connect it to your existing computer. All you need to do is update your computer with the latest multitouch software to take advantage of the latest touch-screen technology.

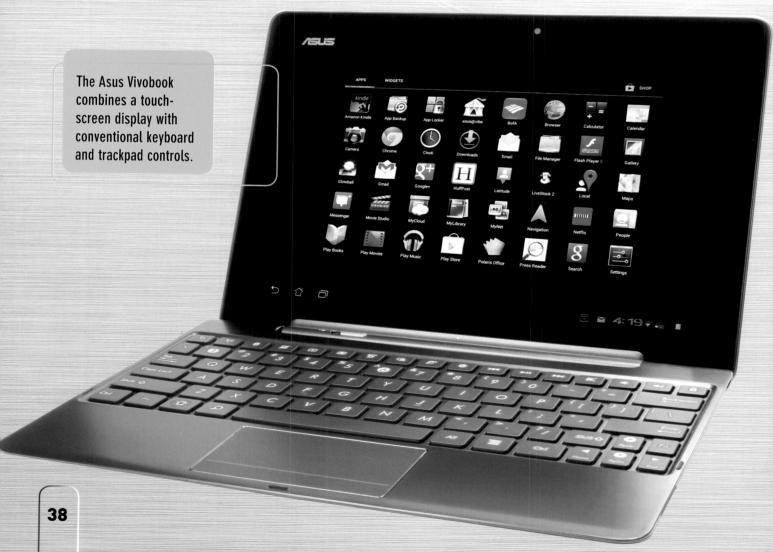

The Asus Vivobook combines a touch-screen display with conventional keyboard and trackpad controls.

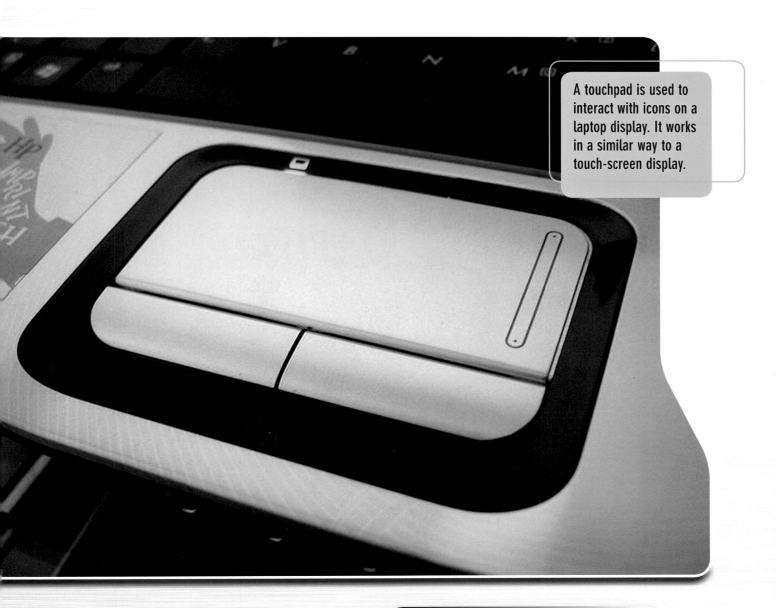

A touchpad is used to interact with icons on a laptop display. It works in a similar way to a touch-screen display.

Multitouch software

Microsoft Corporation has built-in multitouch technology in its operating systems – the computer programs that control how the computer works. Microsoft's operating system, Windows 8, comes with a range of new features. For example, most multitouch systems work with two-finger control. Windows 8 supports apps that work with up to five fingers, making them much more interactive.

CONNECTIONS

Multitouch monitors come with two cables to connect to a PC — a standard monitor cable and a USB cable to enable the touch-screen functions. You can buy a touch-screen monitor and connect it to a standard PC in this way. Once it is connected, you can download the Windows 8 operating system and you will have a touch-screen computer!

CHAPTER FIVE:
THE FUTURE OF TOUCH SCREENS

Touch-screen technology has come a long way in a short time. Some exciting future developments in computing include gesture control to allow people to use computers without touching them at all! Another new development is tactile touch screens, which rely on a technology called haptics.

Gesture control

The next step in touch-screen technology is gesture control, which extends the idea of touch-screen technology. Instead of swiping or tapping on a screen, you might be able to control a computer by simply clicking your fingers, flicking your wrist or pointing at the display.

The Xbox Kinect uses motion-sensor technology to play interactive games.

Motion sensors

Games consoles, such as the Nintendo Wii, are leading the way with gesture control. These devices use motion-sensor technology to control the action on the screen.

Nintendo's Wii Remote is a controller that works using an accelerometer. This device measures the way the player's hand moves while he or she plays the game. The accelerometer feeds this information back to a sensor mounted on the display, which re-creates the movements on the screen.

Microsoft's Kinect system works using an infrared sensor and camera to track the movement of people playing the game. Kinect also uses speech recognition so people can control the game with their voice.

GORILLA ARM

Gorilla arm is the name given to a side effect of using touch-screen technology for too long, when the user's arms being to ache and feel tired. Some people think that this might lead to the downfall of touch-screen technology in the future. However, others say that there is nothing to be concerned about.

Current research

Researchers hope to develop gesture control so they can build computers that do not require any mechanical controls. In the future, they believe computers will be able to recognise facial expressions, body language and complex hand gestures, such as sign language.

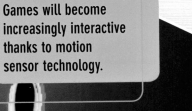

Games will become increasingly interactive thanks to motion sensor technology.

The Nintendo Wii uses a remote and a Nunchuk to convert the movement of your hands into actions on the screen.

NEW DEVELOPMENTS

Many new developments may result from the boom in touch-screen technology. Touch screens of the future may offer new and exciting ways for people to interact with computers.

Tactile touch screens

One exciting development includes tactile touch screens that create different textures on the surface of the screen. For example, touch screens of the future could re-create the feel of objects they display. So you might feel the texture of fur by touching an image of an animal on the screen.

Can you imagine touching a screen and feeling what you can see? Tactile touch screens hope to recreate this sensation.

Flight simulators use haptics to recreate the experience of flying a real aeroplane.

Haptics

As far-fetched as feeling textures on a screen may sound, researchers are developing this idea with a technology called haptics. In fact, this technology already exists in flight simulators and video games, where the controller vibrates to feel exactly like action on the screen. Engineers have also used haptic technology to design tactile 'buttons' on touch-screen devices such as smartphones and tablet computers.

Bendy screens

Another new touch-screen development is the idea of flexible touch screens that act like a sheet of paper and can bend around corners. This idea could be used to develop electronic devices that people can wear, such as touch-screen watches or clothing.

HANDS-ON HAPTICS

One of the most important applications of haptic technology is in education and training. Research has shown that the sense of touch is very powerful. People respond better to learning when they can interact with and touch the objects they are learning about.

A BRIGHT FUTURE

A few decades ago, touch-screen technology was found only in science fiction books and films. Today, it is difficult to imagine a world without touch screens. They are everywhere – in our homes, banks, shops and restaurants, cars and aeroplanes and in the workplace.

There are thousands of smartphone apps. Thanks to touch-screen technology, they are simple to use.

Common technology

The first touch screens were expensive. Scientists invented and used them for special electronic equipment in big research laboratories. Over time, the cost of touch screens fell. Today, many everyday electronic gadgets have touch screens to control them, from smartphones and tablets to games consoles and sat-nav systems.

Ease of use

Touch-screen technology has really changed the way people interact with electronic devices. Most people find it easier to point at an icon on a screen than to use a keyboard and mouse. Touching a screen feels more natural to people and makes these devices quicker and easier to use.

Into the future

Touch-screen technology has moved quickly in the last ten years. What does the future hold for the touch screens of tomorrow? Scientists have already developed tactile touch screens. These high-tech devices have screens that mimic different textures, such as rough and smooth. Future touch screens may also combine with other technologies, such as virtual reality (see box below), to make electronic gadgets even more interactive for the user.

VIRTUAL REALITY

In the future, people may use senses other than touch to engage with computers and other electronic equipment. For example, you might use these devices in a 'virtual world', using eyeglasses and sensors in your clothes to interact and control what you see.

Touch screens are all around us. What do you think the future holds in store?

GLOSSARY

accelerometer a device that measures acceleration (the rate of increase of speed over time)

app short for application software, a program that tells a computer or other electronic device to do something

atoms tiny particles that make up matter

driver software a computer program that allows different electronic devices to 'speak' to one another

electricity energy that arises from the movement of charged particles

electronic circuits networks of electronic parts connected by conductors

ergonomics the science of making machines easier for people to use

gesture control controlling a machine through movements or facial expressions

haptics a new technology that involves the control of machines through touch

hard drive part of an electronic device that stores information

icon a small picture on a screen that allows people to interact with computers and other electronic equipment

infrared light a form of light energy with a slightly longer wavelength than the visible light we can see

Internet the worldwide network of computers that provides e-mail and web pages

kiosk a self-service machine that sometimes includes touch screens so people can use them, for example, to buy tickets

light-emitting diode (LED) a tiny device used in electronics as a light source

microprocessor a device that processes all the information in an electronic device

operating system a computer program that controls how a computer works

particle accelerator a machine that accelerates atoms and other tiny particles to very high speeds

patents legal documents that protect inventors' ideas

PDA shot for personal digital assistant, an electronic personal organiser

polyester clear, hard plastic sometimes used to make the outer covering of a touch screen

reflector material that reflects light

smartphones mobile phones that have some of the features of personal computers

stylus a pen-like instrument that can be used to control some touch-screen devices

tablets small, portable computers contained within flat screens

transducer an electronic device that changes energy from one form into another

satellite navigation system a system that uses a series of satellites in orbit around Earth to map the location of objects on the surface of the planet

virtual keyboard a keyboard that appears on the touch screen and is used to enter information into a computer – just like a normal computer keyboard

FOR MORE INFORMATION

Books

Computer Eyewitness Guide. Dorling Kindersley, 2011.

Gadgets, Games, Robots, and the Digital World. Dorling Kindersley, 2011.

Gilbert, Sarah. *Built for Success: The Story of Apple.* Franklin Watts, 2013.

Websites

The Touch Screen Museum technology guide explains how touch screens work and where they are used.
www.dmccoltd.com/english/museum/touchscreens/around/Automotive.asp

Find out how the best-selling touch-screen device, the iPhone, works at:
http://electronics.howstuffworks.com/iphone.htm

The popular How Stuff works website explains the technology behind tablet computers.
www.howstuffworks.com/tablets/tablet.htm

INDEX